VOWS

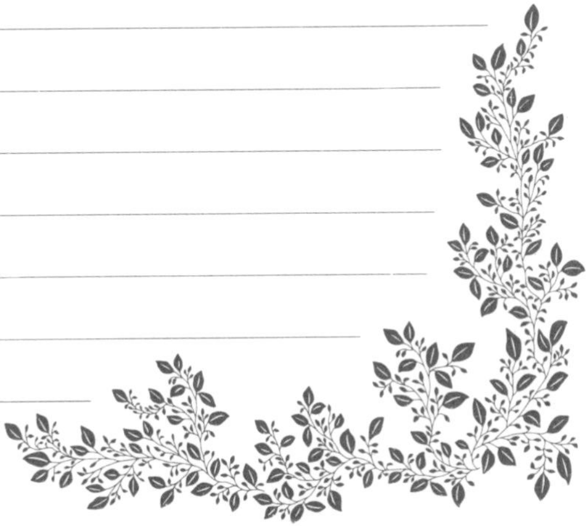

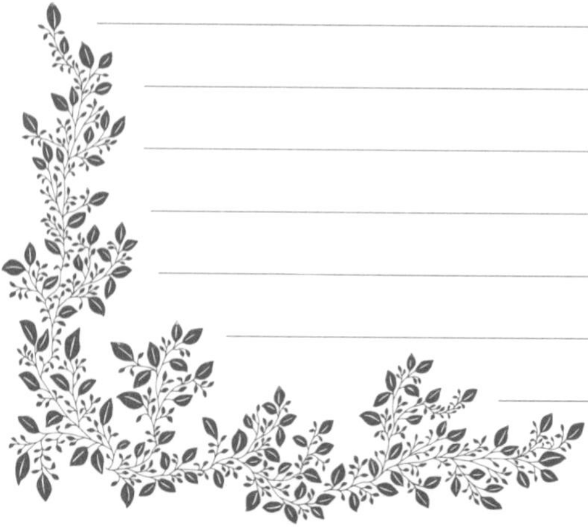

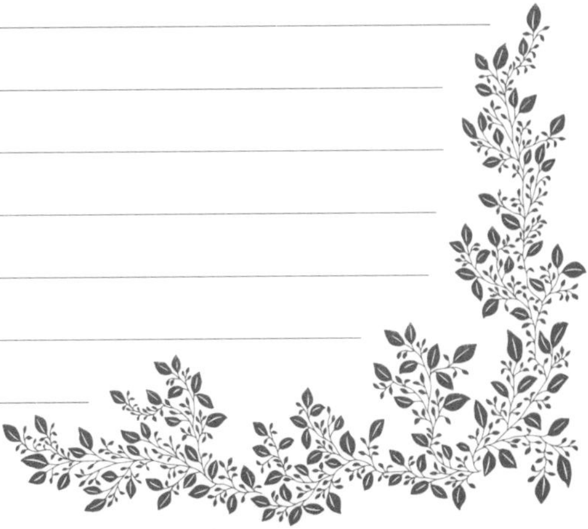

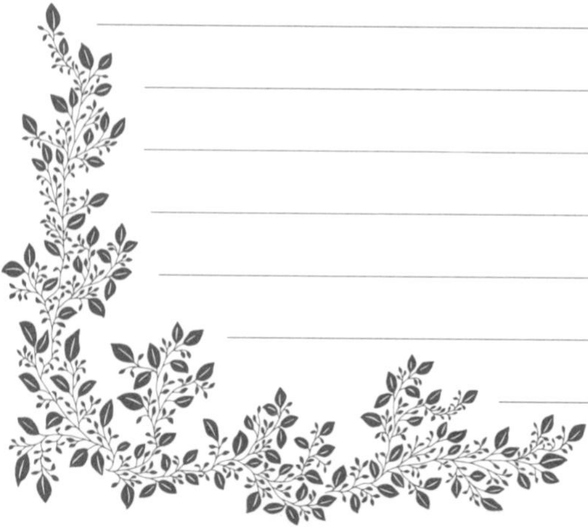

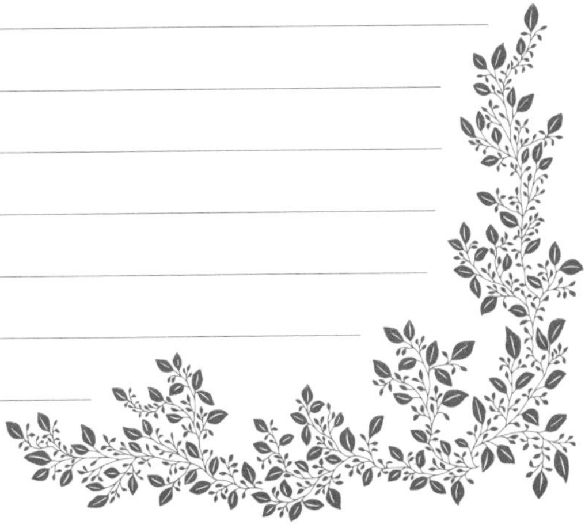

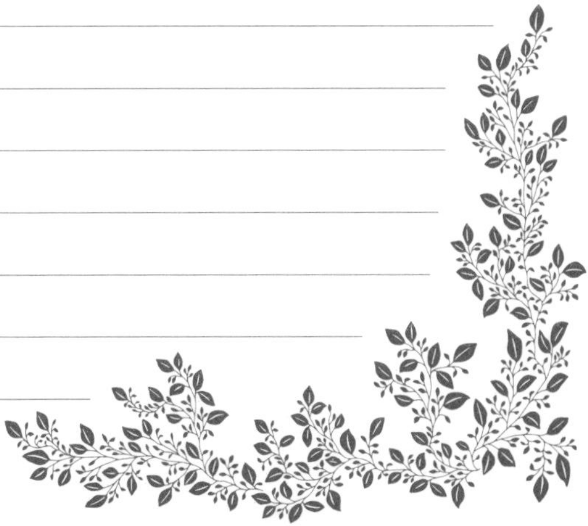

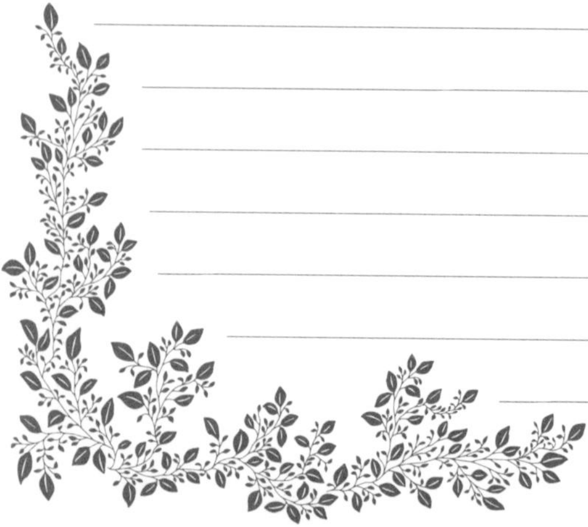

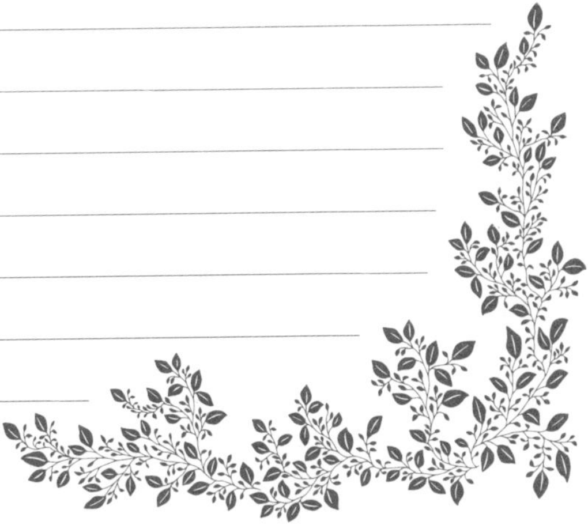

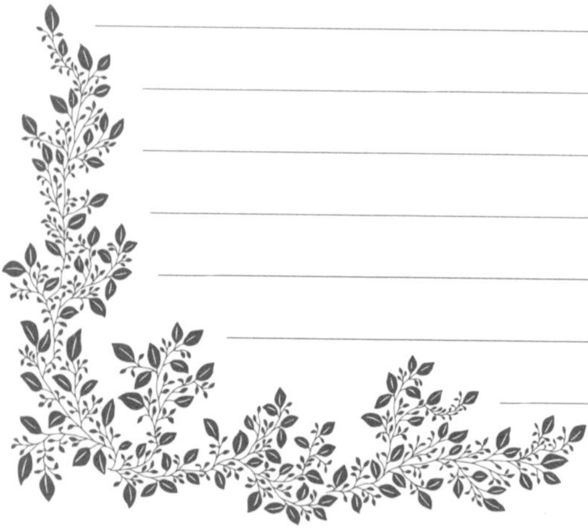

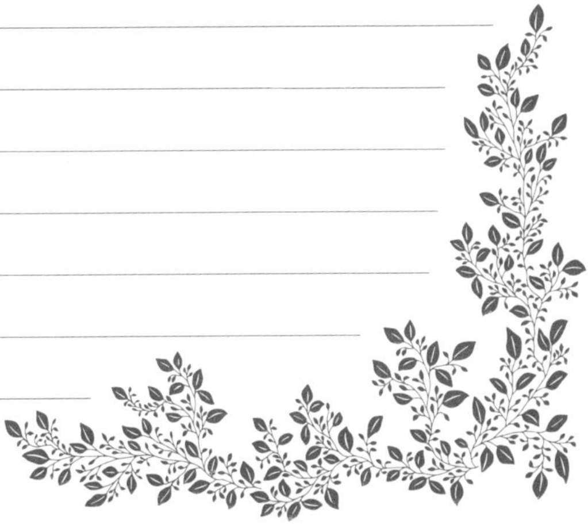

Paige Tate & Co.

ISBN: 9781958803240

Printed in China

KORIE HEROLD

WWW.KORIEHEROLD.COM

Paige Tate & Co.

ISBN: 9781958803240

Printed in China

KORIE HEROLD

WWW.KORIEHEROLD.COM

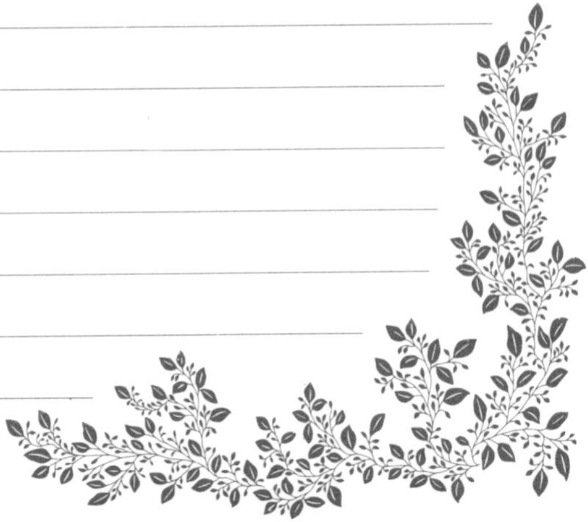

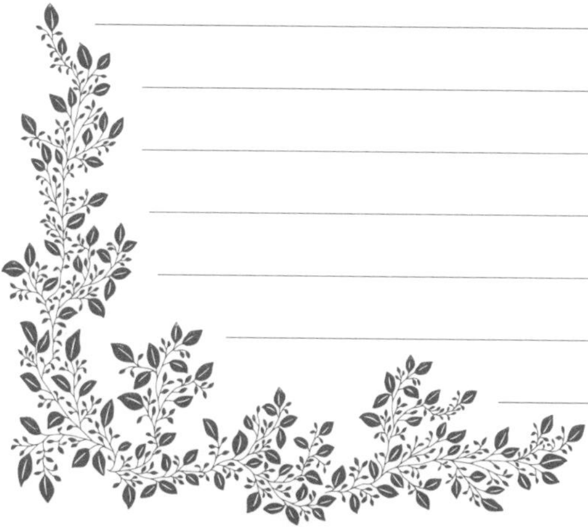

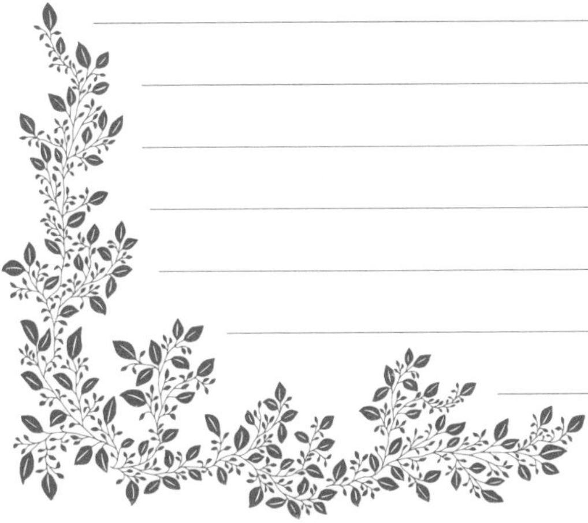

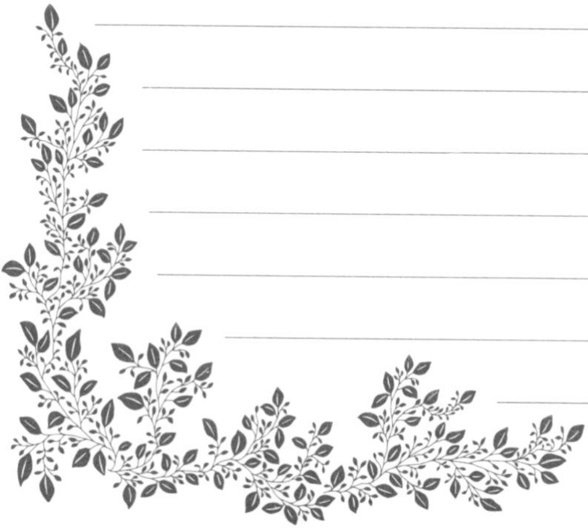

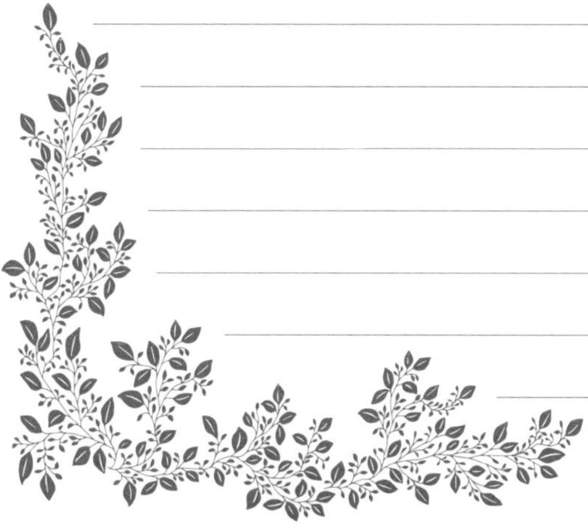

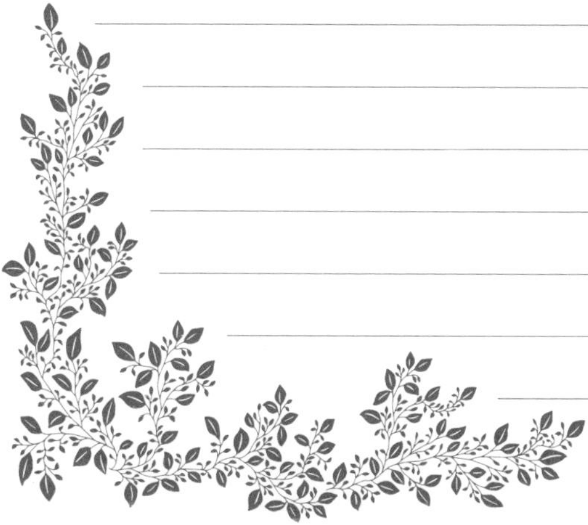

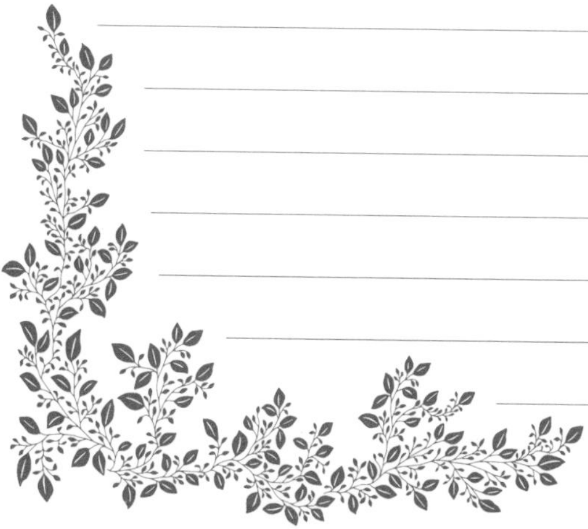

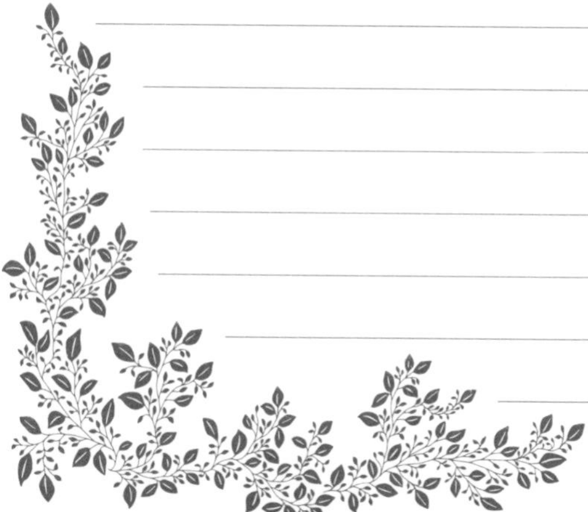

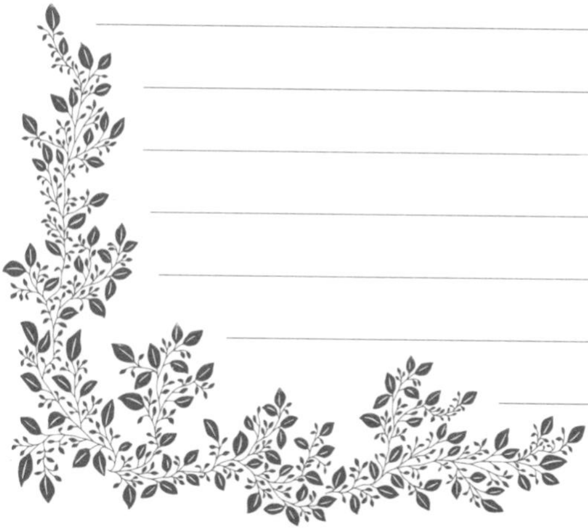

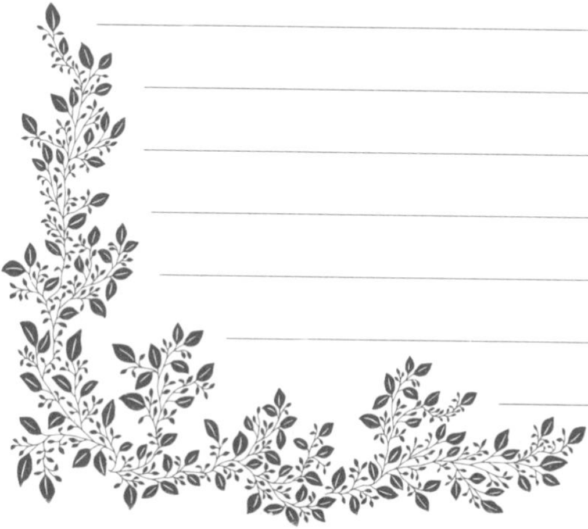

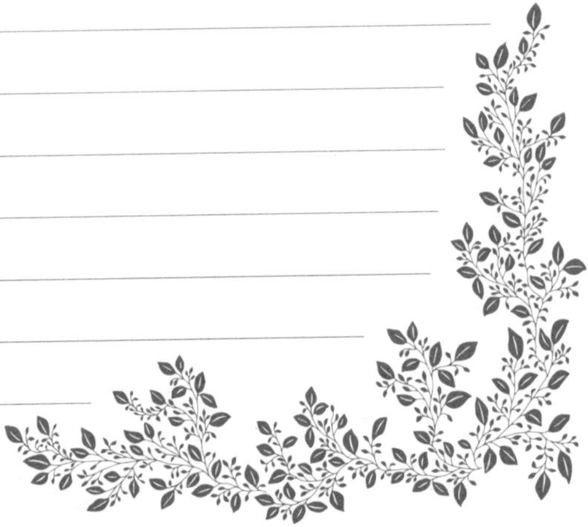

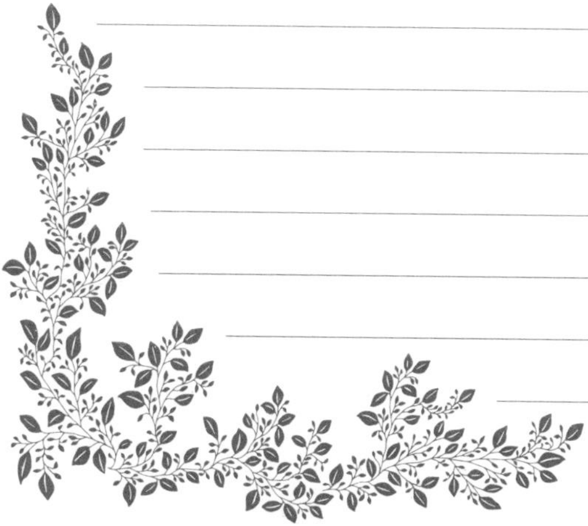

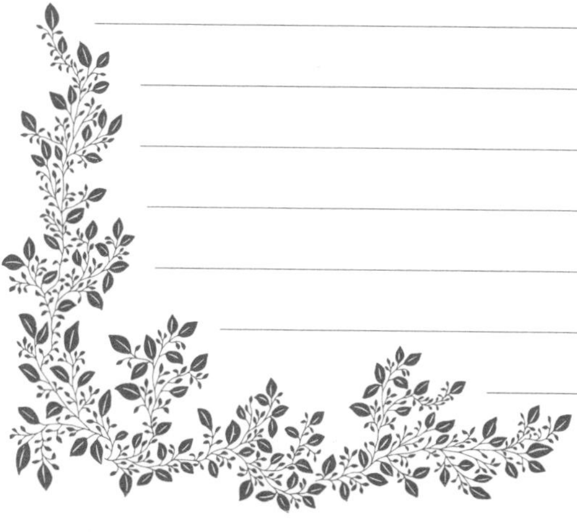

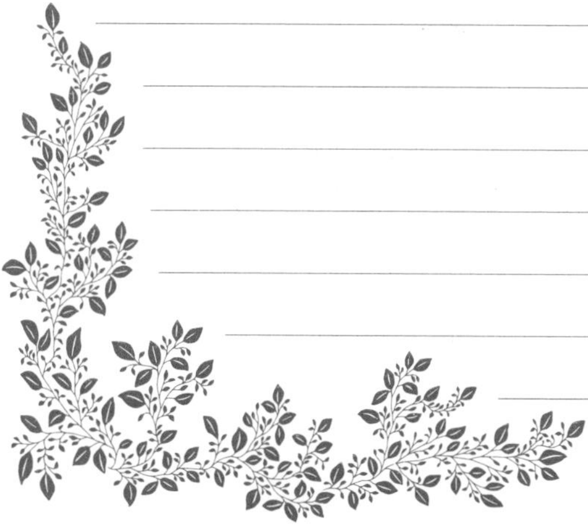

VOWS